Timeless Thomas

How Thomas Edison Changed Our Lives

Menlo Park, New Jersey, Laboratory

West Orange, New Jersey, Laboratory

For my agent, Lori Nowicki,
who has a few great ideas of her own

Special thanks to Paul Israel, Leonard DeGraaf, Leslie Barretta, and Na'Heim Thomas

ISBN 978-0-545-72765-5

Published by Scholastic Inc., 557 Broadway, New York, NY 10012, by arrangement with Henry Holt and Company, LLC. SCHOLASTIC and associated logos are trademarks and/or registered trademarks of Scholastic Inc.

12 11 18 19/0

Printed in the U.S.A. 40

First Scholastic printing, April 2014

Watercolor on Arches cold-press paper was used to create the illustrations for this book.

Timeless Thomas

How Thomas Edison Changed Our Lives

GENE BARRETTA

SCHOLASTIC INC.

Have you ever thought about inventing something of your own? You're never too young to try.

Thomas Alva Edison began experimenting when he was just a boy. That's right. It was the beginning of a life dedicated to improving the world with his brilliant ideas and inventions.

But Thomas couldn't do it alone. When he grew up, he gathered a large team of scientists, engineers, mechanics, and artisans in Menlo Park, New Jersey. Together, they started the first research and development laboratory in the world. It became known as the Invention Factory.

Later, a second lab was built in West Orange, New Jersey. It was even bigger and busier. These were the sites of his greatest successes and his most valuable failures. Edison used his failures as a necessary part of inventing. He once said, "I know several thousand things that WON'T work." And he would always try again.

Present Day

We can now record any sound we like and save it. This was not possible before Edison.

Edison's Lab

Edison's tinfoil phonograph was the first device to record sound and play it back. It was a major scientific breakthrough and earned him his nickname—The Wizard of Menlo Park. That's pretty impressive for a man who was partially deaf.

TO RECORD:
Cover the cylinder with tin. Rotate it and speak into the horn.

The voice vibrates a needle on the end of the horn.

The vibrating needle makes small sound grooves on the rotating tin.

TO LISTEN:
Stop and place the needle back to the start. Rotate the cylinder.

The needle rides over the sound grooves and plays your recording.

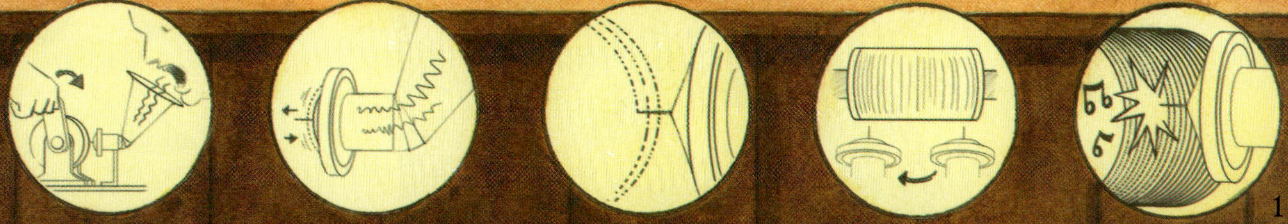

Present Day

If Thomas Edison were alive today, he would be fascinated by the many ways we listen to recorded sounds. It all started with his phonograph.

Edison's Lab

Edison constantly improved on his phonograph so it could have multiple purposes. Models were designed for homes and public arcades.

Phonographs were also introduced to offices as the first dictation machines. It became possible for office workers to record spoken information, save it, then play it back when they were ready to copy it down.

A small phonograph was built for the first talking doll.

Present Day

Today the telephone is the easiest and quickest way to contact someone. The telephone was first invented by Alexander Graham Bell. Yet Edison improved it.

Edison's Lab

All telephones have a transmitter (where we speak) and a receiver (where we listen). Edison created a transmitter that was powerful enough to send our voices much farther and make them sound much louder.

Edison introduced the word "hello" as the official telephone greeting. Alexander Graham Bell wanted us to use "ahoy, hoy."

Present Day

The photocopier and the tattoo needle seem to have nothing in common.

Yet they were both based on Edison's electric pen—it was the first motorized copier.

Like a tattoo machine, the electric pen contained a small needle that moved in and out. While writing a message, the needle poked holes in the paper to create a stencil. Ink was spread over the stencil to make copies.

Lewis Carroll, the author of *Alice's Adventures in Wonderland*, was a big fan of the electric pen.

Present Day

Need a battery? Take your pick. Today they are made in many shapes and sizes.

Edison's Lab

One of Edison's biggest successes was his nickel-iron storage battery. It was originally created to power an electric car. But since the electric car didn't catch on, he found many other important uses for it.

For example, Edison's battery was used to power . . .

Buoys

Local delivery trucks

Railway cars and signals

Boats and submarines

Rural homes

Miners' lamps

Present Day

Before vending machines became a popular stop for tasty treats . . .

When members of our government cast a vote, they use very basic voting machines.

The X-ray machine is a common way to photograph the inside of our bodies.

Edison's Lab

Edison had the idea of a large-scale vending machine for the urban poor. It featured coin-operated openings across a wall, each one filled with necessities, like coal and farm produce.

Thomas Edison invented a vote recorder for the government. It was his very first patent. Having a patent means you legally own an invention. Over the course of his career, he was awarded 1,093 patents for his ideas.

Edison's fluoroscope was the first example of X-ray technology. It generated bright and fast images. The basic design is still used today.

Present Day

When we hear the word *Hollywood*, we think of bright lights, big movies, and glamorous celebrities.

But did you know that Hollywood is not the birthplace of the movies? The movie industry was essentially started at Edison's lab. His goal was to offer an experience that "does for the eye what the phonograph does for the ear."

Edison's Lab

So Edison created the first motion picture camera—the Kinetograph. The technology was similar to our modern movie cameras. He also built the first movie studio and called it the Black Maria (ma-RYE-ah) because it resembled a police patrol wagon with the same nickname.

Movie lights did not exist yet. So they opened the roof and used the sunlight. As the sun moved, the studio followed it on a revolving track.

Present Day

Today we can watch our favorite movies on a big screen, at home, or even on our phones.

Edison's Lab

The first movies were shown on Edison's Kinetoscope, which did not project images onto a screen. It was built for peephole viewing—one person watched at a time.

Edison's Kinetophone was the first projector to show movies with synchronized sound. The projector was connected to a phonograph. It wasn't perfect, but it was the first.

When people watched movies for the first time, they were amazed to see even the simplest movements, like . . .

A woman dancing | A man sneezing | A boat in the water | A man posing | A rooster walking

Present Day

It's very possible you may have walked on pavement created in Edison's factory. Edison's cement was used for all sorts of construction, like dams, buildings, roads, sidewalks, and the original Yankee Stadium. He even built a few cement houses. Oddly enough, his successful cement business was the result of a major failure.

Edison's Lab

Edison originally built a special factory to remove iron ore from rocks, then use the ore to make iron briquettes for steel production. He and his team designed remarkable machinery for the project.

The iron ore project failed. But instead of being discouraged, the team changed their plans and used the rock waste sand to manufacture cement. Success!

It was necessary to roast the large supply of cement mixture. So Edison designed a roasting kiln that was 150 feet long—more than twice the size of average kilns!

Present Day

When you chat with your friend on a computer, you send electronic messages across wires and radio waves—just like the old telegraph machines did. Edison began working as a telegraph operator in his teens.

Present Day

Today we use radio waves to transmit all types of signals, including those from mobile phones, radar, television, and radio.

Edison's Lab

He eventually improved telegraph technology with machines that could not only send messages faster, but could also send several different messages on the same wire and in opposite directions.

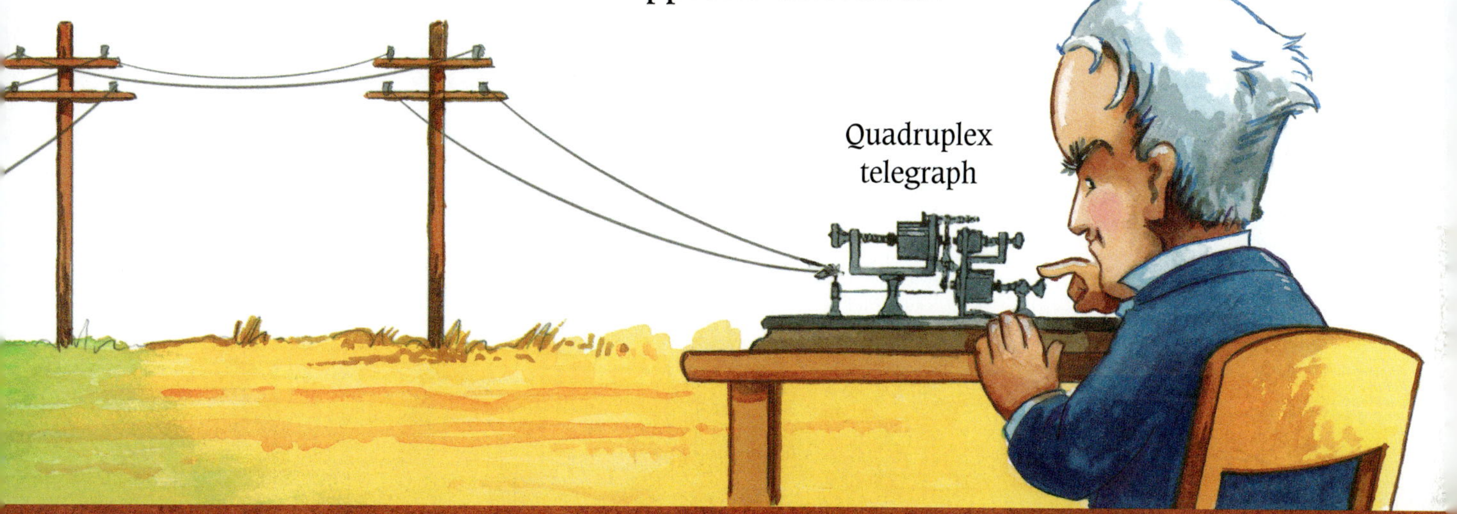

Edison's Lab

Thomas Edison was among the first to discover radio waves in the air, although at the time, he couldn't fully explain his discovery.

Present Day

Our quality of life has certainly been improved by the extraordinary work of Thomas Edison and his colleagues at the labs. Think about this: bedtime stories would be very different today if it were not for Edison's most popular and important invention—the incandescent lightbulb.

Edison's Lab

After thousands of experiments, Thomas Edison produced a lightbulb that was perfect for homes and offices. It was sturdy, safe, and bright. It also burned a long time. This breakthrough ultimately changed the way we live. And it was also excellent for shadow puppets.

Present Day

Edison's bulb worked as part of an elaborate light and power system large enough to power an entire city. He once told a newspaper that he would be the first person to light up a portion of New York City. It took four years of hard work, but he kept his word.

Edison's Lab

Edison built the first large electric generator and power system on Pearl Street in Manhattan. The key feature was its ability to send electricity to many different locations at once. It became the model for the future.

Present Day

So every time you turn on a light, think of Thomas Edison and remember everything he gave us.

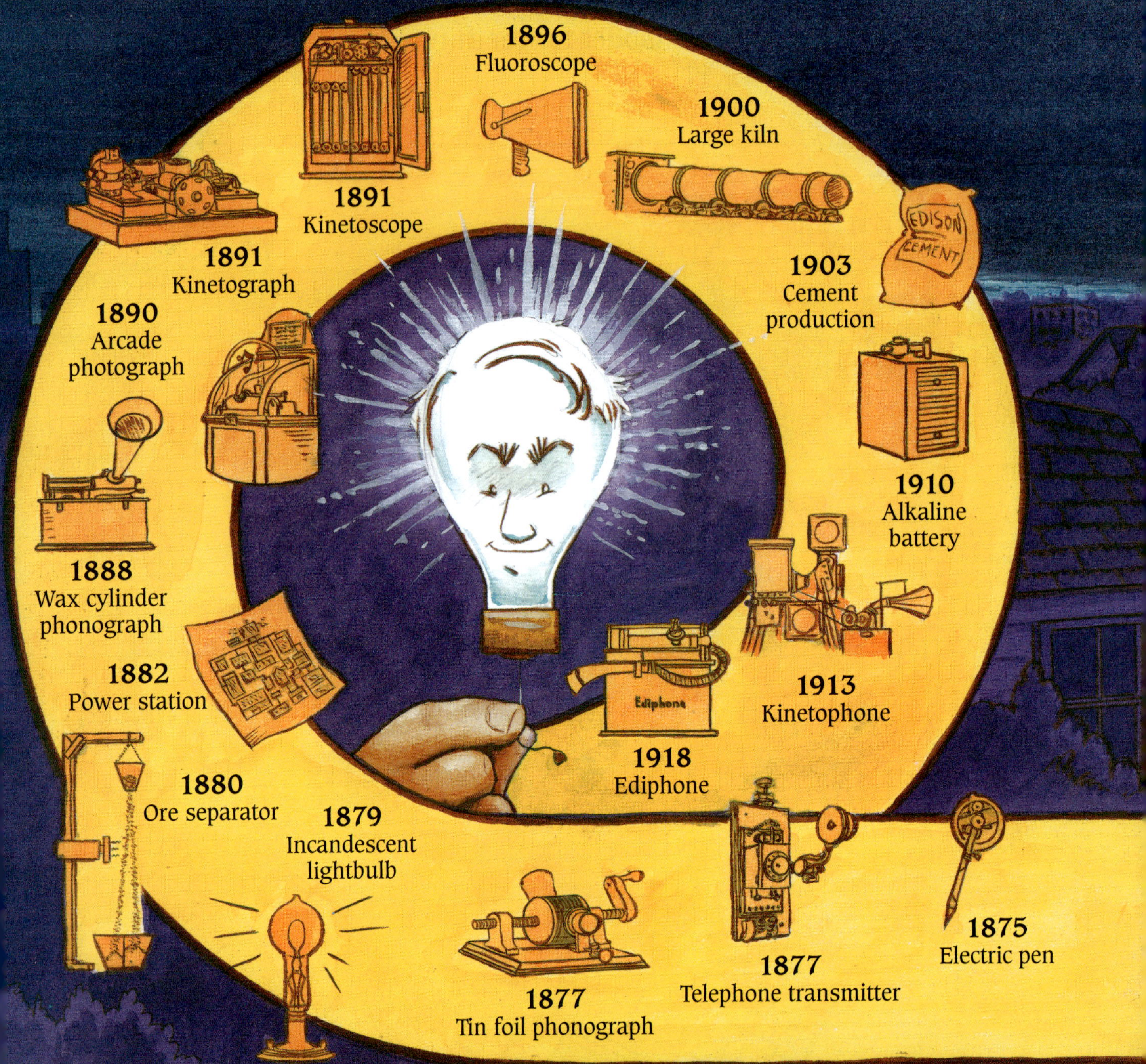

Edison's Lab

One of the greatest tributes to his work came on the day of his funeral in 1931. President Herbert Hoover asked the entire country to honor Edison by turning off the lights for a minute of darkness.

People everywhere honored a lifelong career filled with important inventions and innovations—a career that began in the small home laboratory of a young boy with lots of ambition and dreams.

Edison Employees

Here are brief bios of the employees who appear in the book. They were often hired to perform a variety of duties for several projects.

Ludwig Boehm. Born in Germany. Glassblower and electrician. Worked at length on the incandescent bulb. (page 8)

Francis Jehl. Chemist. Worked on the electric light and power station. Traveled to Europe to introduce the Edison light system. Wrote the book *Reminiscences of Menlo Park* based on his early diary. (page 8)

Alfred Haid. German. Early employee and chemist at Menlo Park. (page 8)

John Kruesi. Swiss. Head machinist and inventor. When Edison sketched an idea on paper—like the first phonograph—Kruesi was responsible for building it and making it work. (page 11)

Jonas Aylsworth. Chemist. Tested and developed many materials for phonograph discs and cylinders. (page 13)

Walter Miller. Sound recording expert. Started just after the West Orange lab opened and stayed there his entire career. (page 13)

James Adams. Assisted Edison on several telephone experiments. (page 15)

Charles Batchelor. British. One of Edison's closest laboratory assistants and business partners over a thirty-year period. (page 17)

Walter E. Holland. Chief engineer at the Edison Storage Battery Company. (page 19)

W. K. L. Dickson. Staff photographer. Very active in the development of the first motion picture camera and early projectors. (page 23)

Charles H. Kayser. Inventor and mechanic. Also involved in the development of the first motion picture equipment. (page 23)

Fred Ott. Machinist. Best known as the star of one of Edison's earliest films, *Fred Ott's Sneeze*. It was a three-second movie of Fred sneezing! (page 25)

William Heise. German. Director of photography. Helped build the Black Maria. Developed early lighting and framing techniques for filmmaking. (page 25)

John Ott. Principal instrument and model maker. Superintendent of the machine shop. He was Fred Ott's brother. (page 25)

William H. Mason. Chief engineer at the cement plant. He later invented a popular hardboard called Masonite. (page 27)

Walter Mallory. Helped Edison convert the failed ore factory to a productive cement factory. (page 27)

Francis Upton. Mathematician. Worked mainly on the electric light and power system.(page 31)

John Lawson. Chemist. Conducted extensive experiments on the lightbulb. (page 31)

Charles Clarke. Engineer. Designed commercial power stations and dynamos. (page 33)

Samuel Insull. British. Edison's private secretary and financial manager. Helped develop electric power and distribution stations. (page 33)

Thomas Trivia

- As a boy, Edison had only a few months of formal education.
- At a young age, Edison rescued a telegraph operator's child from the path of an oncoming train. As a reward, the operator formally taught Edison how to work the telegraph.
- Edison proposed to his wife, Mina, in Morse code. She accepted in Morse code. (Morse code is the alphabet of electronic dots and dashes used when sending a message by telegraph.)
- Edison nicknamed two of his children Dot and Dash.
- The Menlo Park lab had a pipe organ and, for a brief time, a real pet bear cub.
- The first recording ever made was Edison speaking the nursery rhyme "Mary Had a Little Lamb."
- Edison worked very long hours at the lab. It was not unusual to find him napping on one of the worktables.
- In 1914, a huge fire destroyed more than 15 of Edison's factory buildings in West Orange, New Jersey. Fortunately, the laboratories were untouched.
- For the last three years of his life, Edison's entire diet was a pint of milk every three hours. He did this to help soothe his stomach troubles. But the lack of nutrients and fluids led to major health problems.
- Edison's last major project was to research and grow natural rubber in the United States. At the time, rubber came from other countries.
- Edison and his staff filled more than 3,000 notebooks with ideas.

Bibliography

BOOKS

DeGraaf, Leonard. *Historic Photos of Thomas Edison.* Nashville: Turner Publishing Co., 2008.

Israel, Paul. *Edison: A Life of Invention.* New York: John Wiley & Sons, Inc., 1998.

Pretzer, William S., Ed. *Working at Inventing: Thomas A. Edison and the Menlo Park Experience.* Baltimore: Johns Hopkins University Press, 1989.

WEBSITES

The Thomas Edison Papers (Rutgers): http://edison.rutgers.edu

Thomas Edison National Historical Park: http://www.nps.gov/edis

DVD

Biography: Thomas Edison. A&E Networks.

Menlo Park, New Jersey, Laboratory

West Orange, New Jersey, Laboratory